anythink

D0687186

NO LONGER PROPERTY OF
ANYTHINK LIBRARIES/
RANGEVIEW LIBRARY DISTRICT

anythink

ADVENTURES IN NATURE

BIRDS

Cath Senker

PowerKiDS press™

Published in 2016 by
The Rosen Publishing Group, Inc.
29 East 21st Street, New York, NY 10010

Cataloging-in-Publication Data
Senker, Cath.
Birds / by Cath Senker.
p. cm. — (Adventures in nature)
Includes index.
ISBN 978-1-5081-4575-2 (pbk.)
ISBN 978-1-5081-4576-9 (6-pack)
ISBN 978-1-5081-4577-6 (library binding)
1. Birds — Juvenile literature.
2. Birds — Identification — Juvenile literature.
I. Senker, Cath. II. Title.
QL676.2 S46 2016
598—d23

Copyright © 2016 Watts/PowerKids

Series Editor: Sarah Peutrill
Series Designer: Matt Lilly
Picture Researcher: Kathy Lockley
Illustrations: Andy Elkerton

Picture Credits: Dreamstime.com/Amber Estabrooks 29CR,
Ampack 4, Anton Harder 17TR, Arman Bilge 29CL, Brandon
Holmes 23(c), Brian Lambert 13BR, Deepta 23BR, Epstefanov
6BL,Iouri Tomofeev 17BL, Jennifer Thompson 23(e), Lee
Amery 17TL, Louise Rivard 24B, Mallios 13TL, Manuel Novo
22, Maxim Blinkov 5, Menno67 23(b), Mikelane45 16T, Nikolay
Dimitrov 13C, Operative401 14BL, Sandi Mitchell 19, Spychala
Pawel 17TC, Thomas Dobner 14R, Thomas Langlands 17BR,
Willi Van Boven 16B. Istockphoto/Andy Farrer/lensflairuk 13RC,
RyanVincePhotography 25. Shutterstock.com/Ainars Aunins 7CR,
Aksenova Natalya 21BR, Arturo de Frias contents page, 10CL,
Bildagentur Zoonar GmbH 18, Borislav Borisov 29C, Chris Hill
13BL, davemhuntphotography 21BL, Dionisvera 7BR, Eric Isselee
21CL, Erik Mandre contents page, 10CR, Erni 23 (d), (f), Euro
Spiders 8, FloridaStock contents page,10TR, Georgios Alexandris
10CR, Glenn Young 28, Gotzila Freedom 13LC, iliuta goean 23(a),
Karel Gallas 13BCL, Keneva Photography 10BR, LianeM 6TR,
Lucy 20 Menno Schaefer 13BCR, 24TR, Miao Liao 21CR, Michael
Woodruff 12, Miroslav Hlavko 6BR, Natalia Davidovich 29BR,
Ondrej Prosicky 27, Paul Reeves Photography 6LC, Peppersmint
Front cover, Peter Gudella 29TL, Peter Schwarz 7CL, Schankz
7BCL, Sekar B 26, solkahar 14TL, Stefano Garan 10L, taviphoto
7TR, T-gomo 7BL, Tsekhmister 7BCR, Vetapi 7TL, Vishal Shinde
23g, Zhao jian kang 21TR.

All rights reserved. No part of this book may be reproduced
in any form without permission in writing from the publisher,
except by a reviewer.

Manufactured in the United States of America

CPSIA Compliance Information: Batch #BW16PK: For Further Information contact
Rosen Publishing, New York, New York at 1-800-237-9932

Can you find SIX Birds' EGGS hidden on the pages?

Clara is out looking at birds. Can you find her?

There are lots more puzzles in this book. You can solve them by reading the text or by looking closely at the photos. The answers are on page 30.

Contents

The great bird hunt

So you're interested in birds – fantastic! Bird watching, or birding, is a popular pastime and it's easy to get started. This book gives you some basic information about birds and where to find them, along with puzzles and outdoor activities.

Birds live in different kinds of places, so begin exploring in your town or village. Look for a good "local patch," with a variety of habitats to attract different kinds of birds. An area with a pond or lake, trees, and fields is ideal.

Watching a seagull in flight near a lake.

Get prepared

Some basic items will come in handy. You'll need a pair of binoculars that are light and small enough to wear comfortably – compacts might be good. Find a field guide with illustrations of birds and information to help you to identify them. Use a notebook or digital tablet to record details of the birds you see.

Always record details of the birds you see.

Bird watching

Look at this local map. Where would be good places to see birds?

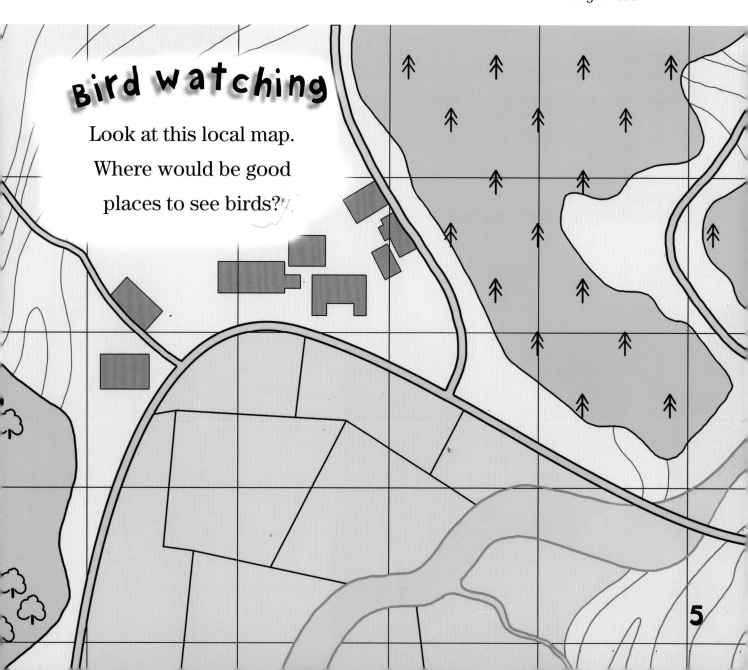

Types of beaks

When you're looking at a bird, examine its beak. It could be long, thin, short, or wide. Birds' beaks are adapted to the kind of food they eat.

duck

Warblers feed high in the trees. They have a thin, pointed beak, which is good for picking insects off leaves and twigs.

warbler

Woodpeckers also feed on trees. They have a strong beak for pecking holes to reach insects living under the bark and for breaking nuts.

Mallards are common ducks you'll see on ponds and lakes. The edge of their beak is fringed to strain plants, seeds, and small animals from the mud and water.

Birds of prey, such as buzzards and eagles, catch and kill live animals, such as birds, fish, and rodents. They have a sharp, hooked beak to attack their victims.

buzzard

woodpecker

Beaks and breakfast

Find the right food below for these hungry birds.

woodpecker

duck

eagle

warbler

pond plant

ants

acorn

mouse

feathers for flying

Feathers grow out of a bird's skin just like hair grows on our heads. Birds' feathers gradually wear out or get damaged. New feathers grow and push out the old ones.

Birds take good care of their feathers so they are fit for flying and insulate their body. They preen to remove dirt and spread preen-gland oil through their feathers to waterproof them. Then they shake to get rid of the dirt, creating a cloud of dust. Birds also bathe regularly in water or dust.

Grouse

Tertials are closest to the body

Primaries are long flight feathers

Secondaries are shorter flight feathers

Feathers overlap so they are streamlined for flight and keep out wind and rain.

Camouflage

Birds' feathers can act as camouflage to hide from predators or prey.

Can you spot six birds in this picture?

THE BIRD HUNT CHALLENGE

Feathers

Wearing gloves, look for feathers in the park and figure out which bird they come from.

In flight

Of all the animals, birds are the flying champions. They fly by flapping their wings, steering mainly with their tail. Watching how birds fly helps you identify them.

Eagles and most hawks have long, broad, soaring wings. Their long primary feathers stretch out to catch thermals (upward currents of hot air).

bald eagle

raven

Crows, ravens, and blackbirds have elliptical wings, perfect for short bursts of rapid flight. Other birds have high-speed wings for flying extremely fast over long distances – watch ducks, falcons, and terns. The fastest flier is the peregrine falcon, which can reach 200 miles per hour (320 km/h) – as fast as the highest-speed train!

gull

albatross

Birds with active soaring wings depend more on the wind currents to fly. Their long, narrow wings allow them to soar for a long time. Albatrosses, gannets and gulls have active soaring wings.

tern

peregrine falcon

Which bird?

Identify each bird by its wing type.

a

b

c

d

e

f

THE BIRD HUNT CHALLENGE

Flight

Watch birds to learn the different ways they fly.

Nests for baby birds

These swallows are nesting in a hole in a tree.

Most birds build nests, where they lay eggs and often care for their young.

Falcons, owls, and many shore birds build simple nests. The plover, a wading bird, makes a scrape nest – a hollow in the ground to keep eggs from rolling away. Falcons often nest in holes in a tree or on cliff ledges.

Lots of birds make more complex nests using small stones, mud, twigs, leaves, and other plant fibers. They weave the materials or "glue" them using mud or spiders' webs. Blackbirds and many other perching birds make cup nests in trees by weaving grass and twigs together. Most elaborate of all are the woven hanging nests built by the weaver birds of Africa.

Find my nest

Which bird uses each nest?

a

b

c

d

THE BIRD HUNT CHALLENGE

Build a nest

Gather natural materials and weave them together or stick them together using mud.

falcon

weaver bird

plover

blackbird

Try not to disturb birds' nests and never take eggs from them.

Parks and gardens

How can you attract birds to your yard at home or school? Some birds may come without invitation! Pigeons will nest in a chimney, under roofs, and in gutters. Robins love to nest in sheds.

This pigeon is nesting in a roof.

Encourage birds by providing food for them, especially in the cold winter months. Some birds are ground feeders. Ask permission to scatter bird food on the lawn or patio. Keep an eye out for thrushes, robins, and blackbirds. Sparrows, tits, and finches will visit a seed feeder – hang it where cats can't reach it. Tits, nuthatches, and woodpeckers will cling on to a mesh feeder to snack on nuts or bird food.

blue tit

great tit

American robin

You can put out a bird bath to provide your visitors with water for drinking and washing.

14

Helping birds

Which of these bird feeders and bird baths are in a good place?

a

b

c

d

e

f

g

THE BIRD HUNT CHALLENGE

Make a bird bath

Place a large, clean plant pot on an old upside-down bucket. Put pebbles in it and fill it with fresh water.

In the countryside

In the countryside, you may spot birds you don't see in the city. Look out for house wrens along fencerows or woodlands at the edges of a field, starlings racing across fields, American crows eating grain in fields, and red-tailed hawks soaring overhead.

Always take an adult with you on nature walks and stay on the footpaths.

Starlings

Barn owl

It's good to learn common bird songs to help you recognize birds – listen to them on the North American Bird Sounds website. In the northeast, listen for Eastern meadowlarks and other songbirds, which build their nests in hayfields and meadows. In the early morning or late evening, you might hear the screeching of a barn owl.

16

Silhouette puzzle

Match the bird silhouettes to their pictures.

b

c

a

d

e

wren

sparrow

crow

starling

great tit

Deep in the woods

Woodlands may have deciduous trees – which lose their leaves in the winter – or coniferous trees, which keep their leaves. They might have both. Deciduous or mixed woodlands are the best for birding.

It can be hard to spot the birds among the leaves. Every so often, stop, wait, and watch. Keep an eye out for birds moving from branch to branch or from tree to tree. You may see finches, tits or warblers. On tree trunks, woodpeckers or nuthatches might appear.

greenfinch

Draw birds

It's easy to draw birds if
you start with egg shapes.

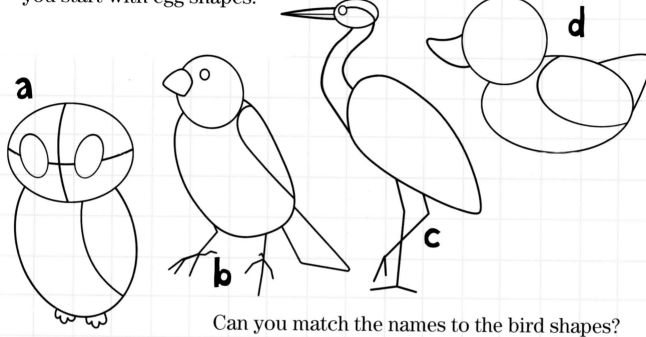

a

b

c

d

Can you match the names to the bird shapes?
One name is missing. What do you think it is?

heron   sparrow   owl

Different levels

Scan at different levels: on the
ground, you might spot thrushes and
wrens. Check for sheltered, sunny
patches and clearings out of the wind
– insects cluster here, which provide
food for birds. Birds also gather at
pools of water to drink and wash.

A thrush looks for food on the woodland floor.

Lake Visitors

Be Careful! Lake banks may be slippery.

Mallards and Canada geese on a lake.

Lakes and ponds are great places for seeing a variety of birds. Birds feed over, on, and under the water. Trees and bushes on the banks of the pond or lake provide food and shelter. Check for warblers and herons feeding at the water's edge. There may be kingfishers perching in trees – look out for them swooping low over the water.

Terns fly low over the lake to catch insects in the air or pick them off the surface of the water, while the grebe plucks insects off the surface. Mallards, geese, and swans swim on the lake. They duck their heads down to feast on plants, seeds, and small animals in the water.

Webbed feet

Have you noticed how swimming birds usually have webbed feet? As they paddle, webbed feet push away more water than feet with separate toes. (You keep your hands together when you swim for the same reason.) When the birds get out of the water, webbed feet allow them to walk easily on mud.

Chinese geese

Whose feet?

These birds have got the wrong feet!
Which feet should each bird have?

heron

a

goose

c

kingfisher

b

duck

d

Where the river joins the sea

At estuaries, the river joins the sea. When the tide goes out, it reveals a stretch of mud with lots of worms, crabs, and other invertebrates. They provide plentiful food for birds, including wading birds and others that live near water.

At low tide, keep an eye out for common waders such as sandpipers, curlews, herons, and egrets on the seashore. They have long legs for wading through shallow water, and their beaks are adapted for catching and eating fish and invertebrates. Remember to watch for the tide coming in!

golden plovers

estuary birds

Unscramble the words to find the names of the estuary birds in the pictures.

a naws

b segoo

c lulg

d wulcer

e snadripep

f luckshed

g tormancro

High tide

Visit just before high tide and see if you can identify grebes, ducks, geese, swans, gulls, and cormorants swimming in the estuary. Cormorants dive for fish under the water. Look up to discover flocks of birds in the air too. Keep scanning up and down – birds are constantly on the move!

Sand plovers flock over a beach.

23

At the seaside

On a trip to the seaside, you'll probably notice flocks of gulls. They're not timid, so go up close to get a good view – but watch they don't seize your sandwiches! Beaches and cliffs have big, noisy colonies of puffins, guillemots, razorbills, kittiwakes, or gannets – birds that live in groups. Some birds, including gannets, nest on beaches. Make sure you don't disturb them.

A puffin with a mouthful of fish.

Gannets nesting on the shore.

count the flock

Bird watchers try to estimate the number of birds in a flock. Count a small group of birds. What fraction of the total does this group make up? For example, if it's a sixth, multiply by six to estimate how many birds there are altogether.

Out to sea

Look out to sea with your binoculars and scan for gannets, terns, cormorants, eiders and gulls. Gaze upwards at the cliffs, and, if you're lucky, you'll spot peregrines or kestrels.

Peregrine falcons prey on birds such as ducks.

up in the hills

Hilly habitats are home to several types of birds. When you're hill walking, look for birds perched on fences and boulders. You may see grouse on the ground. Scan the sky for birds of prey soaring over the hillsides, such as eagles, ospreys and buzzards.

bald eagle

Birds of prey are predators. Excellent hunters, they mostly eat small mammals, such as voles and rabbits, as well as birds and fish. They catch them live or find carrion (dead animals). The birds dive extremely fast to catch and kill their prey with their powerful curved talons. Their razor-sharp hooked beak and talons work like a knife and fork, tearing and cutting up food.

Birds of prey, like this goshawk, have keen eyesight and superb hearing.

owl's dinner

Can you spot the owl's prey in this picture?

The birding year

Birds are active all year round. In spring, listen for birdsongs and watch birds carrying leaves and twigs to build their nests. Soon, they'll be flying back and forth with food for their hungry babies. Later, you'll see the young birds, which often look different than their parents.

flock of snow geese

Migrant birds arrive from the south once plants are growing and there are plenty of insects and places to nest. They stay for the summer. At the end of the season, there are fewer insects and many plants are dying, so there's less to eat. Many species, including birds of prey, waterfowl, and perching birds such as thrushes and warblers, fly to the Caribbean and Central and South America for winter.

Swallows gather on telephone lines before migrating from Europe to Africa.

In winter, some birds migrate from colder to warmer areas of North America. White-crowned sparrows migrate from Alaska and the Yukon to the southern USA and northern Mexico.

Bird seasons

Put these pictures from the birding year in order, starting with spring.

THE BIRD HUNT CHALLENGE

Nest boxes

....

Put up a nest box in late winter and see if a bird uses it.

a

b

c

d

Puzzle answers

5 Bird watching

The riverbanks, woods, and fields shown on this map are all good places to spot birds. Birds are all around us so always keep your eyes open to notice them.

7 Beaks and breakfast

woodpecker – acorn
(and seeds and insects)
duck – pond plant
eagle – mouse
warbler – ants

9 camouflage

11 which bird?

a – albatross
b – raven
c – peregrine falcon
d – tern
e – bald eagle
f – gull

15 Helping birds

Bird feeders – the bird feeders attached to the tree (**a**, **d**) are in safe places, where birds can feed without coming to harm. The feeder on the wall (**b**) is too low and **c** is too close to the house and to the cat flap.
Bird baths – **f** is in a good place but **e** is too close to the cat flap where the cat could hide and then catch a bird as it bathed.

17 Silhouette puzzle

a – crow
b – starling
c – great tit
d – wren
e – sparrow

19 Draw birds

a – owl
b – sparrow
c – heron
d – The other bird is a duck

13 Find my nest

a – plover
b – weaver bird
c – blackbird
d – falcon

21 whose feet

heron – d
kingfisher – c
goose – a
duck – b

25 count the flock

Five in the highlighted group, which is a sixth of the flock. 5 x 6 = 30 birds in the flock.

27 owl's dinner

Can you find:
rat
small bird
fish
rabbit

23 Estuary birds

a – swan
b – goose
c – gull
d – curlew
e – sandpiper
f – shelduck
g – cormorant

29 Bird seasons

spring – c
summer – b
autumn – d
winter – a

Glossary

adapted For animals, suited to the place they live or the food they eat.

camouflage The way in which an animal's color or shape matches its surroundings and makes it difficult to see.

colony A group of plants or animals that live together or grow in the same place.

elliptical An oval shape, like an egg.

predator An animal that kills and eats other animals.

preen When a bird cleans itself or makes its feathers smooth with its beak.

prey An animal that is hunted, killed, and eaten by another.

rodent A type of mammal such as a rat, mouse, or squirrel.

habitat The place where a particular type of animal or plant is normally found.

insulate In an animal, to protect the body, for example, with fur or feathers, to prevent heat from passing through.

invertebrate An animal without a backbone.

migrant A bird or an animal that moves – migrates – from one place to another, according to the season.

streamlined A bird with a smooth, even shape so that it can move quickly and easily through air or water.

talon Long, sharp curved nail on the feet of some birds, especially birds of prey.

wader, or wading bird Any of several different types of bird with long legs that feed in shallow water.

waterproof A substance that does not let water through or that cannot be damaged by water.

Index

Websites

PowerKids Press has developed an online list of websites related to the subject of this book. This site is updated regularly. Please use this link to access the list:
www.powerkidslinks.com/ain/birds